Me and my Pet

DOG

Christine Morley and Carole Orbell

Illustrations by
Brita Granström

TWO CAN

In association with
FRANKLIN WATTS

Conceived, designed and edited by:
Two-Can Publishing Ltd
346 Old Street
London
EC1V 9NQ

Art Director: Carole Orbell
Senior Managing Editor: Christine Morley
Additional design: Amanda McCourt and Helen Holmes
Consultant: Lisa Cobb, NCDL Animal Nurse of the Year 1995
Illustrator: Brita Granström
Photographers: Ray Moller, Rocco Redondo
Thanks to Tim Kelly

This edition published in 1996 in association with:
Franklin Watts
96 Leonard Street
London
EC2A 4RH

Hardback ISBN: 1 85434 381 5
Paperback ISBN: 1 85434 382 3

Dewey Decimal Classification 636.7

Printed in Hong Kong by Wing King Tong

Hardback 2 4 6 8 10 9 7 5 3 1

Contents

Your best friend

Owning a dog is fantastic fun. You can take him on long walks, feed and groom him, and in return he'll love you to bits! But to be a perfect dog owner, you need to know a few things about dogs...

Wild wolves

Your dog has a fearsome relative – the wolf. Thousands of years ago, some wolves gave up their wild ways and settled with humans. All the different types, or breeds, of dog you see today are relatives of these tame wolves.

Wolves are the distant ancestors of all dogs.

Most dogs are friendly and like to be cuddled.

Dogs today

In some ways, dogs still behave like wolves. They will track a scent and chase after things that move. They also like to live in groups or packs, and follow a leader. As your dog's owner, you are now his leader!

Perfect pals

If you look after your dog properly, he will become your best friend. He will want to defend his new home against other dogs and strangers. He will also think that you and your family are rather strange-looking dogs!

Give your dog lots of love and attention, and he'll be your friend forever.

Why doesn't she have long ears like me?

Dogs, such as this basset, can smell and hear things that people can't.

All shapes and sizes

Dogs can be as small as a football or as big as you. Some breeds have long silky hair, others have short, curly coats. With so many different types, it can be difficult to choose your favourite!

A hundred-and-one dogs
By letting different dogs breed or have puppies, people have made new types of dog that are good at doing certain jobs, such as herding or hunting. Some types, such as lap dogs, have even been bred to be cute companions.

I'm too big to be a lap dog.

Me too!

Some small dogs were bred to sit on their owner's lap to keep them warm.

I'm not scared of you!

Feeling sheepish

Farmers use dogs to round up their flocks of sheep in the fields. A sheepdog is very obedient. She listens to her master's voice to tell her where to go and what to do.

A sheepdog has to be very fast and quick to keep the flock together.

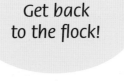

Beware of the dog!

A lot of people use dogs to guard their homes. Although you can buy breeds that are very fierce and bark loudly, even a tiny dog will try to scare off a stranger!

Get back to the flock!

Yippee! I've found you!

Snow rescue

St Bernards are big, strong dogs with furry coats. They are trained to track down travellers lost in snowy mountains.

The right dog for you

Dogs can live for over 15 years, so when you choose one it must be right for you. Think about how much food, exercise and training he will need, and whether you want a puppy or an adult dog.

Boy or girl?

Boy dogs can be livelier and naughtier than girls. They can also be harder to train. If you buy a female, you must check whether or not she has been spayed. This means she cannot have puppies. Male dogs can also have an operation to stop them breeding.

Puppy love

Puppies are very lovable, but until they are trained they can be naughty and messy. Puppies also need to have some special injections from the vet before they can be taken out for walks.

Puppies are cute, but an adult dog can be just as much fun.

Choose me!

To the rescue!

One of the best places to buy a dog is from an animal rescue home. Here you will find all types of dog and the staff can tell you about each one. If you want a particular breed, then you may have to visit someone who breeds them specially.

Home sweet home

It's important that your dog will fit in with your home and family. Some dogs need lots of space to run around in, others are content in a small flat. If you keep other pets, make sure your dog is happy to make friends!

Puppies will play happily with other animals – once they are used to them!

A healthy hound

Choose a dog that is friendly and curious. Check that his eyes are clear and his coat is shiny. Look into his ears to make sure they are clean.

Don't choose a dog that is much stronger than you are. Otherwise he will end up taking you for a walk!

Do hurry up!

Are you ready?

At first, your dog will find his new home a bit strange and he will want to explore every corner. Make sure you are prepared and soon he will make himself at home.

Creature comfort

For the first day, keep your dog in one room. He will sniff around and explore. Make sure he has a comfy bed, fresh water, food and a chewy toy to play with. Leave some paper on the floor, or a litter tray, for him to use as a toilet. Spend as much time as you can getting to know him.

1 food bowl
2 water bowl
3 lead
4 identity tags
5 collar

Giving your dog a special treat will help him settle in.

I'm going to like it here!

Oooops! I've made a splash!

Danger zone!
Dogs, especially puppies, can get up to all sorts of mischief. Some will chew anything, so keep dangerous things, such as disinfectant, soap and electric wires, out of their reach. Put away any valuable ornaments until your puppy is much better behaved.

Always keep your dog away from dangerous roads.

Safe and sound
Before letting your dog into the garden, make sure the gate is locked. Check that there are no gaps in the fence or hedge that he can wriggle through. Fix an identity tag with his name and your phone number to his collar, in case he gets lost.

Bedtime
Just as you need a warm place to sleep, your dog needs his own cosy bed. You can make one from a large, strong cardboard box and a blanket. Or you could buy a bean bag, or a wicker basket. Keep his bed in a quiet corner out of cold draughts and away from his food and water.

I wonder what's out there?

Feeling hungry

Just like people, dogs love their food! They need meat and cereals to keep them strong and healthy, and to make their coats really shine.

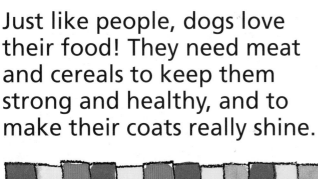

A real dog's dinner!
Although dogs are meat-eaters, they also need other kinds of food to stay healthy. An easy way to make sure your dog is eating properly, is to buy dry or tinned dog food from a pet shop.

Tinned dog food mixed with dog meal makes a healthy dinner.

This beats cornflakes for breakfast!

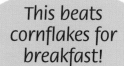

Your dog can't tell the time, but she'll know when her dinner is due!

Tasty treats
To keep their teeth healthy, dogs need something to chew on. You can buy dog chews and bones from pet shops that will do the trick. Never give your dog real bones, as these can splinter.

Don't give your dog too many treats – she will soon get fat.

Feeding time
Most grown-up dogs like to be fed once or twice a day. Puppies need feeding more often. Remember to keep separate bowls for food and water, and clean them regularly. Make sure your dog always has plenty of fresh, clean water to drink.

More greens, please!
You might not expect dogs to like food such as pasta and breakfast cereal, but they do! You can also give your dog scrambled egg, rice, fish, cooked or raw vegetables and fruit, as part of a balanced diet.

The diet starts tomorrow!

Neat and tidy

Dogs are pretty good at keeping themselves clean, but every now and then they may need some help from you!

Brush and comb

Your dog will need his own set of grooming tools. Don't try using your own brush or comb!

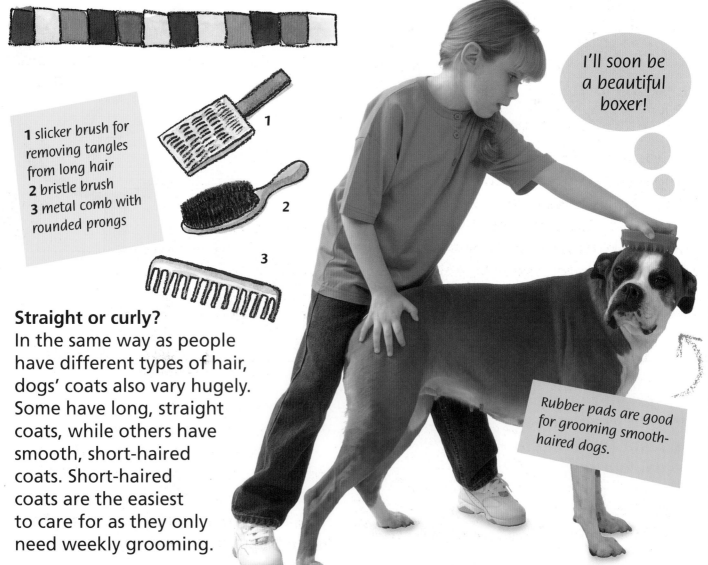

1 slicker brush for removing tangles from long hair
2 bristle brush
3 metal comb with rounded prongs

I'll soon be a beautiful boxer!

Rubber pads are good for grooming smooth-haired dogs.

Straight or curly?

In the same way as people have different types of hair, dogs' coats also vary hugely. Some have long, straight coats, while others have smooth, short-haired coats. Short-haired coats are the easiest to care for as they only need weekly grooming.

Be careful to keep soapy water out of your dog's eyes.

Bathtime

If you groom your dog regularly, he shouldn't need a bath. But if he rolls in something disgusting, a good scrub is the only solution! Use special dog shampoo and rinse it off well. Dry your dog with a towel and finish off with a hair dryer set to a low heat.

Don't use a hair dryer if your dog has itchy skin.

Not too hot – that's just right!

Head first

As part of the grooming routine, you should gently wash your dog's ears and nose, and bathe around his eyes with a piece of cotton wool. Then brush his teeth gently with a special toothpaste for dogs.

Do I need any fillings?

Keeping clean

Most dogs get very excited after they've had a bath and rush around the house at top speed. It's a good idea to keep your dog indoors for a few hours, otherwise he might roll in the mud all over again!

Keeping fit

Dogs need exercise just as you do. Without it, they become bored, restless and may put on weight. Playing games is a good way to exercise your dog – and it's good fun, too!

Play away

The amount of exercise your dog needs will depend on her breed, size and age. Dogs that spend a lot of time indoors should be allowed to run free in a safe place, away from traffic, at least once a day.

Some small dogs need just as much exercise as big ones!

OK, let's play ball!

One more tug should do it!

Walkies!
Dogs love a long walk, even when it's raining! You will have to keep your dog on a lead near traffic, but she will still enjoy the exercise.

Test of strength
Playing a tug-of-war game with a tug toy or an old rag will give both you and your dog plenty of exercise. Don't always let your dog win a game, or she will think she's the boss!

Fetch it!
Dogs love chasing after thrown objects. Toss a ball or frisbee as far as you can and let your dog bring it back to you. Don't be surprised if your dog wants to keep this game going for a while! Only play this game in places where it is safe for your dog to be let off the lead.

Never give your dog a small ball, as she could swallow it.

Training your puppy

Dogs and puppies are clever and eager to please. This makes them really easy to train! Remember to keep your lessons short or your puppy will soon become bored.

Good boy!
You will need lots of patience when training your puppy. Whenever he does something right, make a huge fuss of him and tell him he is a good boy. If he misbehaves, just say "No" to him in a firm voice. Never, ever smack him.

Who am I?
Teach your puppy his name by calling him every time you feed him. Do this when you are playing with him too. Soon he'll learn to come whenever you call his name. Remember to pat and stroke him when he does this.

Here I am!

Call your puppy in a loud, clear voice and he'll come quickly.

Follow my lead

Practise walking your puppy on a lead in your back garden. Put the lead on, then walk forward slowly, calling his name. Never pull him. It will take some time before he can do this, so be patient.

Don't walk a young puppy too far, or he'll get very tired.

Toilet training

When your puppy wakes up in the morning and after meals, he will want to go to the toilet. Watch out for signals, such as sniffing the ground or racing around. Gently pick him up and place him on newspaper or take him outside.

Sitting comfortably

Teach your pup to sit at mealtimes. Stand close in front of him, holding his bowl of food up high. He will have to sit down to keep looking at the bowl. If he doesn't, press his bottom down gently. Say "Sit" a few times, then praise him and give him his food.

But I haven't read the paper yet!

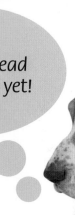

Behaving indoors

Your dog won't be very popular if she chews your shoes or chases the cat all over the house! Teach her some rules to help her get along with everyone at home.

Furry friends

Dogs can get on with other pets, such as cats or guinea pigs, but it may take a while for them to get used to one another. Never leave your pets alone together until you are absolutely sure that they won't hurt each other.

I wonder if kittens like bones too?

No entry

There are some places where your dog will not be very welcome, such as the best armchair. If you find her about to jump on a chair, say "No" firmly, and lead her to her own bed. She'll soon get the message.

Puppies and kittens that grow up together can be good friends.

Eeurrghh!

Use a plant spray or water pistol to tell off your dog – just a little squirt will do.

Naughty dog!

Sometimes your dog will pick up bad habits, such as stealing food from the table. To tell her off, say "No" firmly, and squirt a little water at her with a plant spray. Don't bother to tell her off for something that happened a while ago. She won't remember what she did wrong!

Don't make a fuss of your dog just before you leave – it will make her feel a lot worse.

Home alone

Dogs don't like being on their own for long. If they are lonely, they often bark or howl, or even chew the furniture. When you have to leave your dog alone, rub her favourite toy with your hands, so that it smells of you, then leave it with her. Put the radio on too, so she can hear some human voices!

Behaving outdoors

When you take your dog out, he should be on his best behaviour. Teach him not to bark or growl at other dogs or people, and to sit quietly when you leave him.

Waiting time
Properly trained dogs will sit quietly while their owners walk away. You can practise doing this in your own garden, but never leave your dog tied up for more than a few minutes.

I'm shy
Your dog might feel a bit shy when he meets people or other dogs. To make him feel more brave, keep him close to you and stroke and praise him. It may take a while before he feels more confident, so be patient.

He's so naughty!

I blame the owners.

Sometimes dogs chew things when they are bored, or upset at being left alone.

In the park, keep your dog on a lead until he is properly trained.

Here boy!

Good dogs *always* come back to their owners when they are called. To teach your dog to do this, crouch down, open your arms wide and call him. When he arrives, give him a big hug and lots of pats. He will soon learn that coming back to you is nice!

A neck scratch is the best!

Remember to make a fuss of your dog whenever he comes back to you.

Dog speak

Dogs can "talk" to you in lots of ways, such as by wagging their tails, barking, panting, or even growling. Be a keen dog-watcher and you'll soon learn what they're saying.

Feeling good!

Happy dogs wag their tails and point their ears forwards. To make your dog really happy, scratch her on her back or tummy. She'll be in doggy heaven!

Most dogs love to have their tummies stroked.

Can we go out now?

Attention seeker

Dogs don't like to be ignored. When they want your attention, they bark, howl, or tap you with their paws. They'll even try to sit close to you, putting their faces near to yours!

Eeek – a bunny rabbit!

If your dog is scared, she will flatten her ears and pull her tail down between her legs. She might also growl and bare her teeth. If she is frightened of another animal, she won't look it in the eye. Instead, she might try to hide, perhaps under a table, or even behind you!

Looks like he's hopping mad!

"I'm so excited!"

When your dog is happy, she often jumps with joy. Her ears will prick up and her tail will wag furiously. She will jump up at you, or run around quickly in circles. Perhaps she thinks you're taking her for a walk in the park?

"I want to be alone"

Like people, dogs can get annoyed sometimes. You can tell that a dog is cross by the way she shows her teeth or growls. If she does this, leave her alone.

Don't suddenly disturb an old dog, especially when she is asleep. She may get cross.

Check-up

Most of the time your dog will be bouncing with health. But occasionally he will need some help from you to keep in tip-top canine condition.

Keep a note of all the injections the vet gives your dog.

Feeling poorly

If your dog is off his food, doesn't want to play, or is generally miserable, then he could be ill. Ask an adult to take him to the vet for a check-up. The vet will look in your dog's ears, eyes and mouth and under his tail. Then she'll take his temperature and feel his body for any lumps or bumps.

I'm a sick spaniel!

Rest and relaxation

A sick dog needs a warm and quiet place to rest. Look after him by filling a hotwater bottle with warm water and tucking it in under a blanket in his bed.

I feel silly!

Cool collars

When the vet gives your dog stitches, or puts a bandage on his paw, she might put a large paper or plastic collar on him, too. This is called a Buster or Elizabethan collar. It will stop your dog from scratching his stitches or bandage, so the wound will heal.

Puff flea powder onto your dog's fur, then brush it out again.

No fleas, please!

Even the cleanest dog can catch fleas. You may spot these tiny black insects in your dog's fur. But don't worry, you can get rid of them easily with a spray or powder from the vet. You can even buy special collars to help keep fleas away.

Bits and pieces

You can buy lots of useful and fun things for your dog. Some of these are helpful when you take your dog on holiday, when she's bored, or when the weather is cold.

Boredom busters

If you give your dog lots of toys, she won't get bored. Give her a cuddly toy that she can chew, or a frisbee that she can chase. You can also buy toys with treats hidden inside – your dog will spend hours rooting them out!

Don't let your dog play with your toys, as she might chew them up.

Puppies like soft toys that they can pick up and carry.

On the move

If you're going on a journey, you can take your dog in a special travel box. This will keep her safe and secure, and stop her from running away. Remember to put in a blanket and a small toy she can play with.

I wonder where I'm going?

All dressed up

A dog's fur will keep her warm all year round. But if her hair is clipped, or if it's really cold, she will need a coat for extra warmth. She will look very smart, but watch she doesn't roll in the mud!

Emergency kit

Ask an adult to help you put together a first-aid kit for your dog. You will need some bandages, scissors and cotton wool. Tweezers are also useful for pulling out thorns and splinters from your dog's paws.

Amazing dogs!

Dogs can do some amazing things, from starring in films to exploring the universe!

Fast forward

Some breeds of dog are super-fast. The silky haired Saluki can run up to 69 kilometres per hour, which is faster than a horse can run. A greyhound can beat a horse too.

I love the wind in my ears!

Oodles for poodles

In 1931, a poodle called Toby became the world's first multimillionaire dog. He was left a cool £15 million by his owner Ella Wendel of New York, USA.

Tall tales…

The biggest dog on record was a Great Dane called Shamgret Danzas, who was 105.4 centimetres high.

… and tiny terriers

The smallest dog in the world was a Yorkshire terrier. It measured just over 6 centimetres tall, which is about the size of a matchbox!

Lights, camera, action!
Some dogs have even become famous film stars. Lassie, a rough collie, was the star of eight films. Although Lassie was a girl dog in the film, the part was played by a boy collie called Pal!

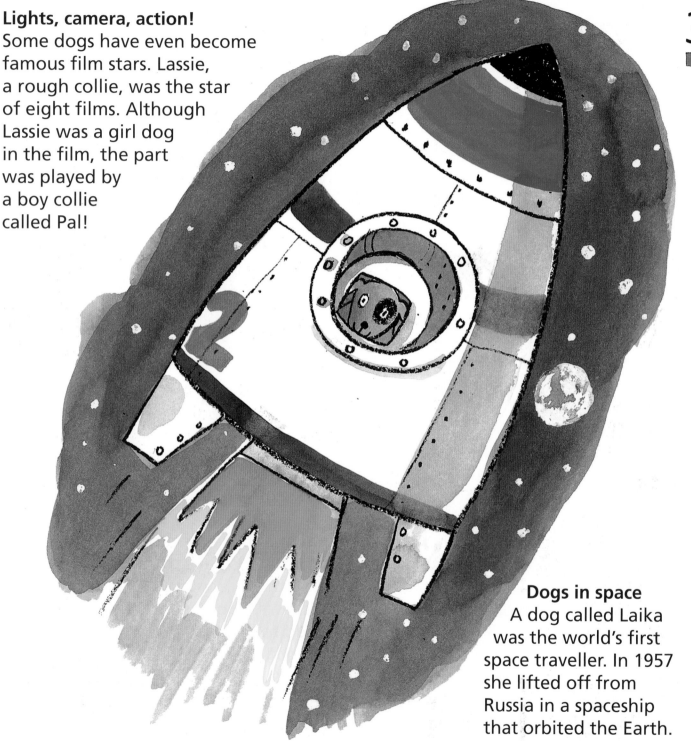

Dogs in space
A dog called Laika was the world's first space traveller. In 1957 she lifted off from Russia in a spaceship that orbited the Earth.

Useful words

bitch The name for an adult, or grown-up female dog. A grown-up male dog is just called a dog.

booster A **vaccination** that a dog should have once a year.

breed A type of **purebred** dog, such as a Labrador or a cocker spaniel.

canine Another word for a dog, or something that is like a dog.

clip If a dog is clipped, it means its coat has been trimmed very short. Dogs with curly coats, such as poodles, often have clipped hair.

crossbreed or mongrel A dog whose parents are different breeds. Mongrels are less likely to suffer from diseases than **pedigree** dogs.

neutering An operation that dogs have to stop them breeding. With female dogs it is called spaying. With male dogs it is called castration.

pack A group of dogs. Every pack has a leader that other dogs obey. When dogs live with people, their owner becomes the pack leader.

pedigree A certificate that belongs to some dogs whose parents, grandparents and great-grandparents are all the same breed. Pedigree dogs can be valuable and are often entered for competitions or shows.

puppy A dog that is less than one year old.

purebred A dog whose parents are the same breed.

vaccinations Injections which dogs have to stop them catching diseases. Puppies need to be injected before they meet other dogs, in case they catch a disease from them.